■SCHOLASTIC

♠♥♣♦♣♠♣♦♣♥♣♠♣♦♠♥♣♠♣♦♠♥♣♠♣♦♠♥

Mega-Fun

Card-Game Math

Grades 3–5

by Karol L. Yeatts

NEW YORK · TORONTO · LONDON · AUCKLAND · SYDNEY
MEXICO CITY · NEW DELHI · HONG KONG · BUENOS AIRES

Teaching *Resources*

To Jim, Terace, Amy, Mom, and Dad
(my royal family)

Cover design by Norma Ortiz
Cover illustrations by Rick Brown
Interior design by Sydney Wright
Interior illustrations by Delana Bettoli

ISBN: 0-439-44855-7
Copyright © 2005 by Karol L. Yeatts
Published by Scholastic Inc.
All rights reserved.
Printed in the U.S.A.

1 2 3 4 5 6 7 8 9 10   40   13 12 11 10 09 08 07 06 05

Contents

Introduction

Cards offer a natural link to math concepts; games motivate students to play again and again. Add them together and you get *Mega-Fun Card-Game Math*—25 skill-building games and activities that help students practice key skills and meet the math standards! With a partner or small group, students will have fun as they practice adding, subtracting, multiplying, dividing, finding averages, rounding, working with fractions and decimals, locating coordinate pairs, using problem-solving and logical reasoning skills, and more.

The games and activities in this book correspond to the standards recommended by the National Council of Teachers of Mathematics (NCTM). For quick reference, the chart on page 6 shows how each activity connects to the NCTM Standards 2000. In addition, playing the games encourages students to build their mental math skills and develop automaticity with computation. *Principles and Standards for School Mathematics* (NCTM, 2000) states that students in grades 3–5 "should develop fluency with basic number combinations" for various operations and that students "should be able to solve many problems mentally." The games and activities in this book provide students with repeated practice to help them achieve those goals.

These games and activities are easy to play and require little or no preparation. Once you have shown students how to play, they'll be ready to play on their own anytime— at lunch, before school, when they have completed other work, and even at home with family members. When students are given opportunities to practice math skills again and again, not only do their skills improve but their confidence and interest levels do, too.

How to Use This Book

The games and activities in this book are arranged by skill, beginning with place value and moving through addition, subtraction, multiplication, division, fractions, decimals, coordinate geometry, probability, and more. To find a game that reinforces a particular skill, refer to the Table of Contents or the chart on page 6.

Most games only require a deck of cards. For some games, students need a reproducible game sheet, markers (such as beans), and pencils. Many of the games offer variations so that you can adapt them as you see fit. In the back of the book, you'll find a reproducible deck of cards so that you can make and replace cards as needed. Have students use a red crayon, marker, or colored pencil to color the hearts and diamonds on the reproducible cards. For durability, photocopy the cards on sturdy paper, round the corners, and laminate them.

Before introducing a game, review the directions and collect any needed supplies. Gather students and model the game by playing it with one or two student volunteers. Once students understand the rules, observe them playing the game together and answer any questions they might have.

Properties of Cards

Review the properties of cards with students—there are 52 cards in a deck and four suits: hearts, diamonds, clubs, and spades. Many of the games in this book call for a deck of cards with face cards and jokers removed. Remind students that the ace is used to represent the number 1. When used, the face cards represent the following values: 11 (jack), 12 (queen) and 13 (king). Jokers are used in some of the games and represent 0. Discuss the importance of shuffling cards.

Order of Operations

Many of the games reinforce the order of operations for solving problems. If needed, remind students of the basic rules when solving problems that include more than one operation. The order of operations rules are as follows:

- If grouping symbols (parentheses) are used, perform the operations within the grouping symbols first.
- Perform multiplication and division in the order it appears, from left to right.
- Then perform addition and subtraction in the order it appears, from left to right.

For example, a player has the following cards:

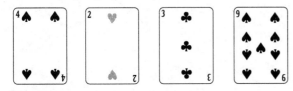

The player creates the following equation without any grouping symbols:

$$4 + 2 \times 3 - 9 = 1$$

The answer is determined by following the order of operations:

- First multiply: $2 \times 3 = 6$
- Then add: $6 + 4 = 10$
- Then subtract: $10 - 9 = 1$

If the player uses grouping symbols, the player could create this equation instead:

$$(4 + 2) \times 3 - 9 = 9$$

- First add: $(4 + 2) = 6$
- Then multiply: $6 \times 3 = 18$
- Then subtract: $18 - 9 = 9$

Before Beginning

Designate a corner or other space in the classroom for playing cards. Remind students to collect all the cards when they have finished and return them to their container. Store the reproducible game sheets and pencils in the game area as well.

Before introducing the games, it is helpful to remind students that the goal of playing is to build math skills, spend time with their classmates, and have fun. If needed, discuss the qualities and benefits of good sportsmanship.

Who Goes First?

Choosing who goes first in a game can be decided several different ways. Brainstorm with students ways to determine playing order. Here are some suggestions:

- Each player draws a card. The player with the greater-value card goes first.
- Each player draws a card. The player with the lower-value card goes first.
- Each player draws two cards and adds their value. The player with the greater sum goes first.
- Each player draws two cards and adds their value. The player with the lesser sum goes first.
- Each player chooses a number from 1 to 10. The top card is drawn from the deck. The player whose number is closest to the card goes first.

Connections With the NCTM Standards 2000

	Number and Operations	Algebra	Geometry	Measurement	Data Analysis and Probability	Problem Solving	Reasoning and Proof	Communication	Connections	Representation
Who's the Greatest?	•						•	•	•	•
Sum 20!	•						•	•	•	•
Card Countdown	•							•	•	•
Plus and Minus	•							•	•	•
As Close as Possible	•						•	•	•	•
Time to Multiply	•							•	•	•
Popular Products	•						•	•	•	•
Factors and Products	•							•	•	•
The Greatest Product	•						•	•	•	•
Dare to Divide	•						•	•	•	•
Your Average Card	•							•	•	•
Fraction Line-Up	•						•	•	•	•
That's One Whole Number	•						•	•	•	•
A Zero Balance	•						•	•	•	•
Dueling Decimals	•						•	•	•	•
Add a Decimal	•							•	•	•
Equation Completed!	•	•					•	•	•	•
Operation Rules	•	•					•	•	•	•
Equation Challenge	•	•					•	•	•	•
Computation Gridlock	•	•					•	•	•	•
Coordinate Pairs			•					•	•	•
Measure Up!	•			•				•	•	•
Possible Chances	•				•	•	•	•	•	•
Magic Card Squares	•						•	•	•	•
Card Detective							•	•	•	•

Who's the Greatest?

Players: 2

Students review place value as they create the greatest four-digit number.

Materials

one shuffled deck of cards with tens, jokers, and face cards removed

The Way to Play

1 One player deals the cards evenly between the players. Players place their cards in a stack facedown in front of them.

2 Each player turns over four cards.

3 Players arrange their cards to make the greatest possible four-digit number.

4 Players read their numbers aloud and decide which number is greater.

5 The player with the number with the greater value wins all the cards from that round and places them in a separate pile.

6 Play continues until all the cards have been used.

7 The player with more cards at the end of the game wins.

Example:

Player 1 has 9,762   Player 2 has 8,421

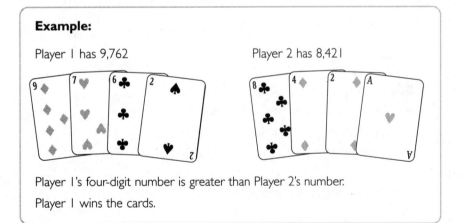

Player 1's four-digit number is greater than Player 2's number.

Player 1 wins the cards.

♠ Variations ♣

- Use five or more cards to create the number with the greatest value.
- Create the number with the least value instead.

Sum 20!

Students create addition problems with sums of 20.

Materials

one shuffled deck of cards with jokers and face cards removed

The Way to Play

1 One player deals five cards to each player and stacks the remaining cards facedown in a pile.

2 Player 1 tries to use some or all of the five cards to create a sum of 20.

- If the player creates a problem with a sum of 20, the player says "Sum 20!" and places the used cards in a separate pile. (Players keep their used cards in their own separate piles.) The player draws cards to replace those used so that he or she has five cards again, and the turn ends.

- If the player is unable to create a problem, the turn ends. On the next turn, the player draws a card and tries again to create a problem.

3 Player 2 takes a turn in the same way.

4 Players continue to take turns until all the cards have been used or until neither player can create a problem. The last player to take a turn may not be able to draw enough cards to replace those used. In this case, the player should draw as many as there are left.

5 When all the cards have been used, players count the cards in their piles and subtract the number of cards remaining in their hands from this number. The player with the greatest number of cards (after subtracting the cards in hand) wins the game.

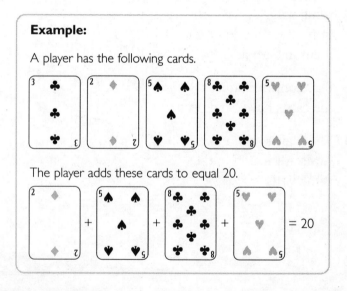

Example:

A player has the following cards.

The player adds these cards to equal 20.

♠ Variation ♣

Change the sum to a different number.

Card Countdown

Materials

two shuffled decks of cards with jokers and face cards removed
Card Countdown Game Sheet, one per player (page 10)
pencils

The Way to Play

1 Each player takes a deck of cards. Players stack their cards facedown in a pile.

2 At the same time, players draw the top card from their piles. Players record the number in the subtract column, subtract the value from 100, and record the difference at the top of the "=" column.

3 Players draw the next card and place it on top of the previous card. Players record the number in the subtract column and subtract the value from the number in the top box. Players record the difference in the next "=" box.

Example:

A player draws a 7 and subtracts 7 from 100 (100 – 7 = 93).
The player draws a 5 and subtracts 5 from 93 (93 – 5 = 88).
The player draws a 10 and subtracts 10 from 88 (88 – 10 = 78).
The game continues until the player reaches 0.

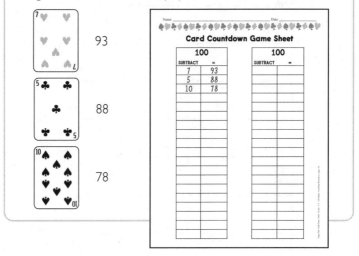

4 Players continue to draw cards, subtract, and record the answers, working as quickly and accurately as possible at their own pace.

5 Players continue until they both reach or go below 0. (For example, 3 – 8 would bring the player below 0.)

6 Players check each other's answers by adding the numbers on the Card Countdown sheet, working from the bottom up. The player with fewer mistakes wins. If both players made no mistakes, the player who finished first wins.

* Include face cards to represent the numbers 11 (jack), 12 (queen), and 13 (king).

Name _____   Date _____

Card Countdown Game Sheet

100	
SUBTRACT	=

100	
SUBTRACT	=

Plus and Minus

Players: 2

Students practice double-digit addition and subtraction.

Materials

one shuffled deck of cards with tens, jokers, and face cards removed
pencils and scrap paper

The Way to Play

1 Player 1 deals five cards to each player. Each player selects any four cards to create the greatest two double-digit numbers possible. Each player adds the two numbers together, records the sum, and places the cards in a discard pile.

2 Player 1 deals three cards to each player. Each player selects any two cards to create the smallest two-digit number possible. Each player subtracts this number from the number recorded in Step 1, records the difference, and places the cards in a discard pile.

3 Player 1 deals three cards to each player. Each player creates the greatest possible two-digit number. Each player adds this number to the number recorded in Step 2, records the sum, and places the cards in a discard pile. This number is the player's score.

4 The player with the higher score wins the game. If at any point a player's score is less than 0, the other player wins.

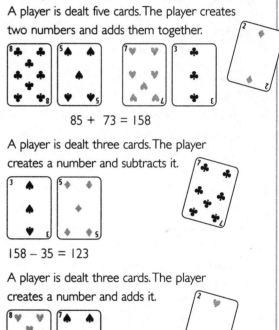

Example:

A player is dealt five cards. The player creates two numbers and adds them together.

$$85 + 73 = 158$$

A player is dealt three cards. The player creates a number and subtracts it.

$$158 - 35 = 123$$

A player is dealt three cards. The player creates a number and adds it.

$$123 + 87 = 210$$

The player's final score is 210.

As Close as Possible

Materials

one shuffled deck of cards (including jokers for 0)
   with tens and face cards removed
As Close as Possible Game Sheet, one per player (page 13)
pencils and erasers

The Way to Play

1. One player deals eight cards to each player and stacks the remaining cards facedown in a pile. Players look at their cards. The object is to create numbers that are as close as possible to the target numbers on the game sheet (5, 25, 50, and 100).

2. Player 1 chooses one of the eight cards and writes the value of the card in a box on the game sheet. The player places this card in a discard pile, draws a new card from the top of the pile, and the turn ends. Players must use one card on each turn. Players may not move the numbers written on the game sheet.

3. Player 2 takes a turn in the same way.

4. Players continue to take turns until they both have finished creating numbers. Players may choose not to fill in the hundreds place in the last line.

5. Players find the difference between the numbers they have written and the target numbers. Players record the differences and add them to find the total difference.

6. The player with the lower total wins.

7. Players may erase their answers and use the sheet again to play another round.

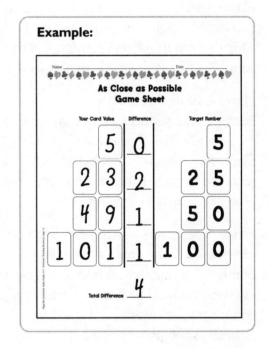

Example:

Name _____ Date _____

**As Close as Possible
Game Sheet**

Your Card Value | Difference | | Target Number

5	0		5
2 3	2		2 5
4 9	1		5 0
1 0 1	1	1 0 0

Total Difference   4

12

As Close as Possible
Game Sheet

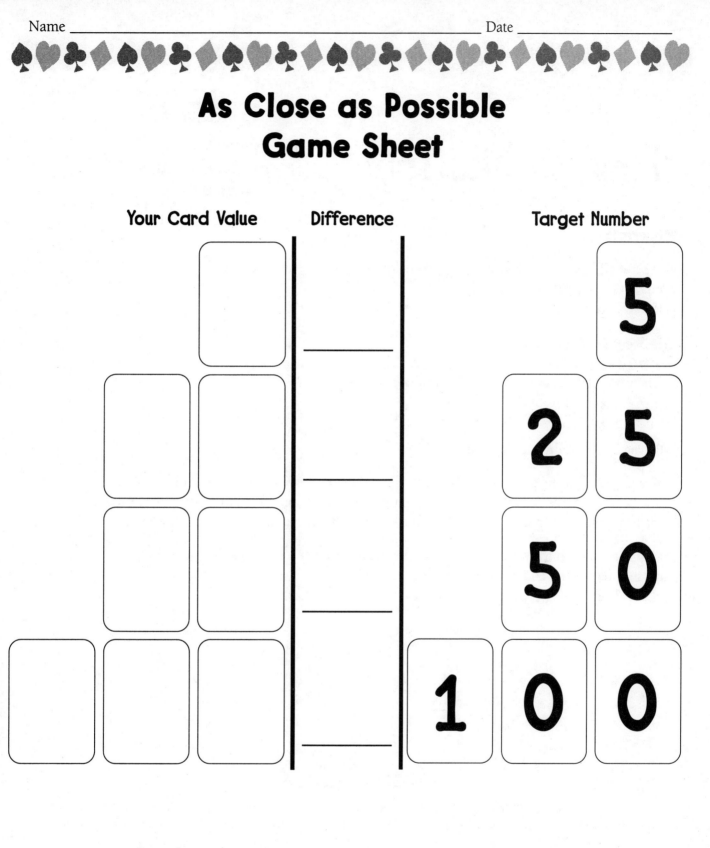

Your Card Value   **Difference**   **Target Number**

5

2   5

5   0

1   0   0

Total Difference _____

Time to Multiply

Materials

one shuffled deck of cards (including jokers for 0) with face cards removed
scrap paper and pencils
calculators (optional)

The Way to Play

1 One player stacks the cards facedown in a pile.

2 Player 1 draws two cards, multiplies the numbers, and says the product.

3 Player 2 takes a turn in the same way.

4 The player with the greater product finds the difference between those two products.
The player records the difference as the number of points earned for the round. The used
cards are placed in a discard pile. If it's a tie, neither player earns points for the round.

5 Play continues in the same way until all the cards have been used. The player with the
most points at the end of the game wins.

Example:
Player 1 multiplies 7 × 5 = 35   Player 2 multiples 10 × 6 = 60

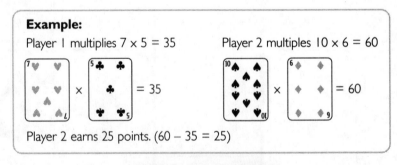

Player 2 earns 25 points. (60 − 35 = 25)

To play a game that reinforces speed, each player draws two cards without looking at
them. Each player turns over one of the cards. At the same time, each player turns over
the second card and multiplies the two numbers. The first player to say the correct
product wins all four cards. If it's a tie, neither player wins the cards. Play continues in
the same way until there are no cards left. The player with more cards wins.

Popular Products

Players: 2 or more

Students practice multiplication facts from 1 to 6.

Materials

one shuffled deck of cards, removing all cards except aces (1) through 6.
Popular Products Game Sheet (page 16), one per player
small markers, such as pennies, beans, or buttons, 10 per player

The Way to Play

1 Players find the products for the factors 1 through 6 and complete the Multiplication Table on the game sheet.

2 Players place their markers on any numbers in the Products Grid. More than one marker may be placed on a number.

3 One player stacks the cards facedown in a pile. The player draws two cards, says the product of the cards, and places the cards in a discard pile.

4 If any player has a marker on that number on their grid, that player removes the marker. (Only one marker may be removed at a time.)

5 The next player draws two cards and play continues in the same way. When all the cards have been played, a player shuffles the discard pile, places them facedown in a pile, and play continues.

6 The first player to remove all 10 markers wins.

Example:

Players complete the Multiplication Table.

Players place markers on any numbers.

A player draws two cards and finds the product.

$3 \times 4 = 12$

The player removes the marker on top of 12.

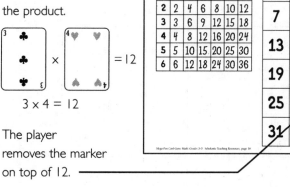

15

Name _____

Date _____

Popular Products Game Sheet

Products Grid

1	2	3	4	5	6
7	8	9	10	11	12
13	14	15	16	17	18
19	20	21	22	23	24
25	26	27	28	29	30
31	32	33	34	35	36

Multiplication Table

×	1	2	3	4	5	6
1						
2						
3						
4						
5						
6						

Factors and Products

Students practice multiplication facts and build an understanding of the commutative property of multiplication.

Materials

one shuffled deck of cards with tens, jokers, and face cards removed
Factors and Products Game Sheet (page 18), one per player
small markers that fit in the boxes on the game sheet, such as buttons or beans
  (transparent plastic markers work well)

The Way to Play

1 One player stacks the cards facedown in a pile.

2 Player 1 draws two cards. These are the factor cards. The player locates the factors on the top and left side of the game sheet. The player places a marker in the box where the two factors meet (the product) and places the two factor cards in a discard pile. A player may place only one marker per turn.

3 Player 2 takes a turn in the same way.

4 Players continue to take turns. If a product box has been covered, a player may not place another marker on it. If a player is unable to place a marker on a turn, the player places the two factor cards in a discard pile and the turn ends.

5 When all the cards have been played, a player shuffles the discard pile and stacks the cards facedown in a pile.

6 The first player to cover three products in a row—horizontally, vertically, or diagonally—wins.

Example:

Player 1 draws two cards.

The player locates the factors 4 and 6 and covers the product (24) with a marker.
The player may place the marker on either product box.

Factors and Products Game Sheet

X	1	2	3	4	5	6	7	8	9
1	1	2	3	4	5	6	7	8	9
2	2	4	6	8	10	12	14	16	18
3	3	6	9	12	15	18	21	24	27
4	4	8	12	16	20	24	28	32	36
5	5	10	15	20	25	30	35	40	45
6	6	12	18	(24)	30	36	42	48	54
7	7	14	21	28	35	42	49	56	63
8	8	16	24	32	40	48	56	64	72
9	9	18	27	36	45	54	63	72	81

Factors and Products Game Sheet

X	1	2	3	4	5	6	7	8	9
1	1	2	3	4	5	6	7	8	9
2	2	4	6	8	10	12	14	16	18
3	3	6	9	12	15	18	21	24	27
4	4	8	12	16	20	(24)	28	32	36
5	5	10	15	20	25	30	35	40	45
6	6	12	18	24	30	36	42	48	54
7	7	14	21	28	35	42	49	56	63
8	8	16	24	32	40	48	56	64	72
9	9	18	27	36	45	54	63	72	81

Factors and Products
Game Sheet

X	1	2	3	4	5	6	7	8	9
1	1	2	3	4	5	6	7	8	9
2	2	4	6	8	10	12	14	16	18
3	3	6	9	12	15	18	21	24	27
4	4	8	12	16	20	24	28	32	36
5	5	10	15	20	25	30	35	40	45
6	6	12	18	24	30	36	42	48	54
7	7	14	21	28	35	42	49	56	63
8	8	16	24	32	40	48	56	64	72
9	9	18	27	36	45	54	63	72	81

The Greatest Product

Students multiply two-digit numbers by one-digit numbers.

Materials

one shuffled deck of cards with tens, jokers, and face cards removed
scrap paper and pencils
calculators (optional)

The Way to Play

1 A player deals three cards to each player and stacks the remaining cards facedown in a pile.

2 Each player uses the three cards to create a two-digit number and a one-digit number with the greatest possible product.

3 The player with the greater product scores a point if the product is correct. Players check each other's work. (Calculators may be used.) If a player could have created a different problem with an even greater product, the player does not score a point.

4 Players place the used cards in a discard pile. A player deals three cards to each player and the next round is played in the same way.

5 When all the cards have been used, the discard pile is shuffled and play continues.

6 The first player to earn 5 points wins.

Example:

A player has these cards:

The player could create the following equations:

65 x 7 = 455
67 x 5 = 335
57 x 6 = 342
56 x 7 = 392
75 x 6 = 450
76 x 5 = 380

The player chooses 65 x 7 = 455.

♠ Variation ♣

Create a problem with the lowest product instead.

Dare to Divide

Students practice division and multiplication.

Materials

one shuffled deck of cards with jokers and face cards removed
scrap paper and pencils

The Way to Play

1 Player 1 deals three cards to each player and stacks the remaining cards facedown in a pile. Player 1 turns over the top two cards in the pile, multiplies them, and says the product. This is the target number.

2 Players look at their cards. Each player gets a point for each card that can be divided evenly into the target number. The player says the division equation for each card that can be divided evenly into the target number. Players check each other's answers.

3 Players place all their cards in a discard pile, draw two new cards for the target number, and play another round in the same way. When all the cards in the pile have been used, a player shuffles the discard pile and play continues.

4 The first player to earn 10 points wins.

Example:
A player draws two cards and says the product.

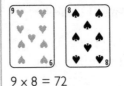

$9 \times 8 = 72$

A player has these cards:

The player earns two points for the following equations:
$72 \div 4 = 18$
$72 \div 6 = 12$

♠ Variations ♣

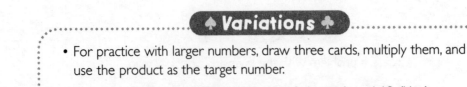

• For practice with larger numbers, draw three cards, multiply them, and use the product as the target number.
• Use face cards to represent 11 (jack), 12 (queen), and 13 (king).

Your Average Card

Students find averages and round to the nearest whole number.

Materials

one shuffled deck of cards with jokers and face cards removed
calculators (optional)
scrap paper and pencils

The Way to Play

1 One player deals four cards to each player and stacks the remaining cards facedown in a pile.

2 Players find the average of their four cards by adding their cards together and dividing the total by four. (A calculator may be used for this step.)

3 Players round their averages to the nearest whole number and record this number on scrap paper. The player earns this number of points for the round.

4 Players place the four used cards in a discard pile.

5 Play continues in the same way. Players shuffle and use the discard pile as needed. The first player to earn 50 points wins the game.

Example:

A player adds the cards.

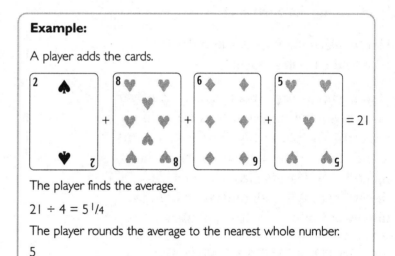

The player finds the average.

$21 \div 4 = 5\frac{1}{4}$

The player rounds the average to the nearest whole number.

5

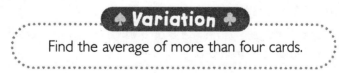

♠ Variation ♣

Find the average of more than four cards.

21

Fraction Line-Up

Players: 2 or more

Students arrange fractions from least to greatest.

Materials

one shuffled deck of cards with jokers and face cards removed

The Way to Play

1. One player deals four cards to each player and stacks the remaining cards facedown in a pile.

2. Players use their cards to create any two proper fractions (the numerator must be less than the denominator).

3. Players place the fractions in order from the least to the greatest fraction.

4. Players check each other's answers. A player earns one point if the fractions are lined up correctly. The player who finishes first earns an additional point if the fractions are lined up correctly. Players place the used cards in a discard pile. When all cards have been used, the discard pile is shuffled and used.

5. The first player to earn 10 points wins.

Example:

A player draws the following cards, creates two fractions, and arranges them in order from the least to the greatest.

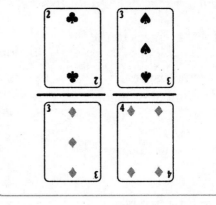

♠ Variations ♣

- Line up the fractions from greatest to least.
- For a more challenging game, use 6 or 8 cards per turn or create both proper and improper fractions.

22

That's One Whole Number

Materials

one shuffled deck of cards with jokers and face cards removed
Fraction Game Sheet, one per player (page 25)
pencils

The Way to Play

1 One player deals six cards to each player and stacks the remaining cards facedown in a pile. Each player takes a game sheet, draws an addition sign in the center box, and writes 1 as the sum.

2 Players try to use four of their cards to form two fractions whose sum is 1. Players place the four cards on their game sheet to complete the equation.

3 • Player 1 takes the first turn. If successful, Player 1 earns a point and places the four cards in a discard pile. The player draws four new cards and the turn ends.

• If Player 1 is unable to create two fractions whose sum is 1, Player 1 draws a card from the pile. The player can either keep the card or discard it. If the player keeps the card, the player must discard a different card. If the player can now create two fractions whose sum is 1, the player does so, following the directions above. If not, the turn ends.

4 Player 2 takes a turn in the same way.

5 Players continue to take turns. When the draw pile runs out, players shuffle the discard pile and this becomes the draw pile.

6 The first player to earn 5 points wins.

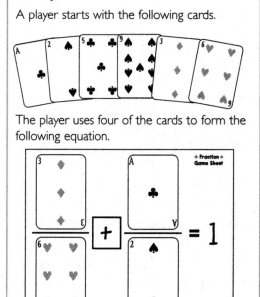

Example:

A player starts with the following cards.

The player uses four of the cards to form the following equation.

23

A Zero Balance

Players: 2

Students form equivalent fractions to complete a subtraction equation.

Materials

one shuffled deck of cards with jokers and face cards removed
Fraction Game Sheet, one per player (page 25)
pencils

The Way to Play

1 One player deals five cards to each player and stacks the remaining cards facedown in a pile. Each player takes a game sheet, writes a subtraction sign in the box, and writes 0 for the difference.

2 Players try to use four of their cards to form two fractions whose difference is 0. On their turns, players place the four cards on their game sheet to show the equation.

3 • Player 1 takes the first turn. If Player 1 is able to complete the subtraction equation, the player earns 1 point and places the four cards in a discard pile. The player draws four more cards and the turn ends.

• If Player 1 is unable to complete the subtraction equation, Player 1 asks Player 2 for a needed card (for example, "Do you have a five?"). If Player 2 has the card, the player hands it over. If Player 2 does not have the card, the player says "Go Fish," and Player 1 draws a card from the deck. If Player 1 is now able to complete the equation, the player does so, following the directions above. If not, the turn ends.

4 Player 2 takes a turn in the same way.

5 Players continue to take turns. When the draw pile runs out, a player shuffles the discard pile and this becomes the new draw pile.

6 The first player to earn 5 points wins.

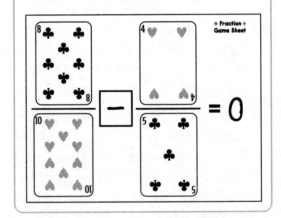

Example:

A player starts with the following cards.

The player asks the other player for a 4 and creates the following equation:

→ Fraction →
Game Sheet

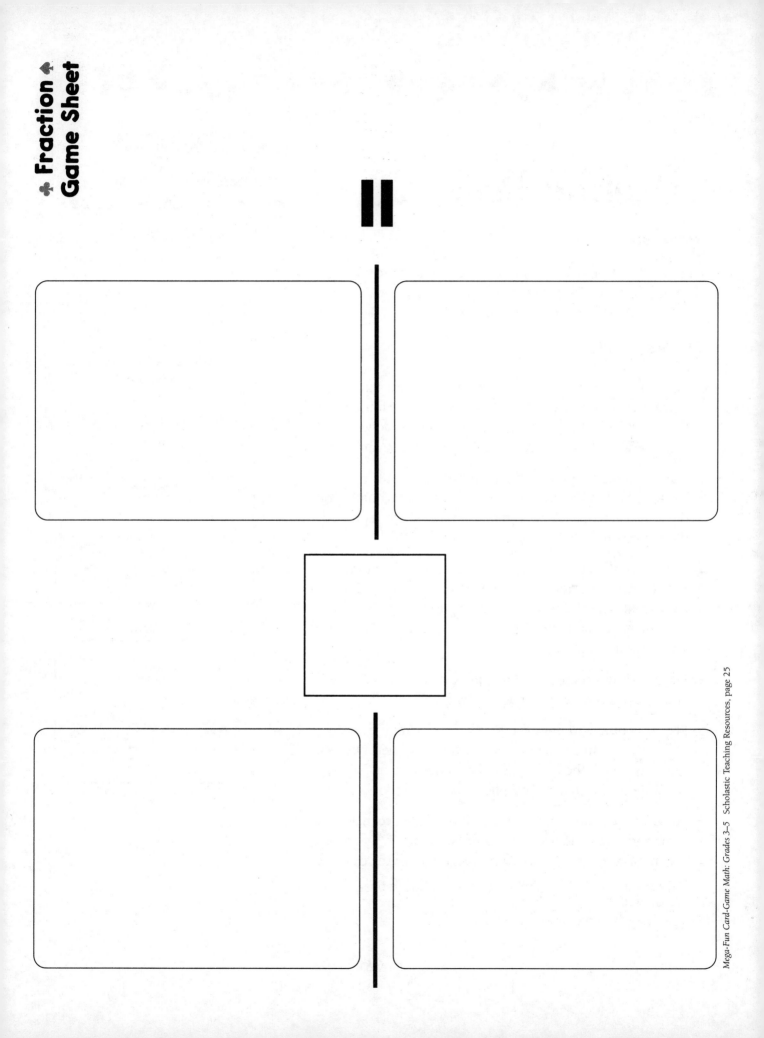

Dueling Decimals

Students create decimal numbers and compare values.

Materials

one shuffled deck of cards with tens, jokers, and face cards removed
Dueling Decimals Game Sheet, one per player (page 27)
small round markers (about the size of a quarter), one per player

The Way to Play

1 Player 1 removes the following four cards of any suit from the playing deck: an ace (1), 2, 3, and 4. Player 1 shuffles these four "decimal point" cards and places them facedown in a row. These cards remain separate throughout the game.

2 Player 1 turns over one of the four cards and reads the number. Each player finds the box with the same number on the game sheet and places a marker in the box to represent the decimal point.

3 Player 1 shuffles the deck of cards and stacks it facedown. Player 1 draws the top card from the deck and places it in any empty box. The object is to create the greatest number. Cards may not be placed in the decimal point box. The other players take turns in the same way.

4 Player 1 draws another card and places it in any box. The other players take turns in the same way.

5 Players continue to draw cards and place them in boxes until each player's game sheet is filled. Players read their numbers. The player with the greatest number earns 1 point. The used cards are placed in a discard pile.

6 To begin the next round, Player 2 shuffles the decimal point cards and turns one over. The game continues in the same way until one player earns 10 points. When all the cards have been used, a player shuffles the discard pile and this becomes the draw pile.

Example:

A player chooses a 3. Players place the decimal point in box 3 on the game sheet.

Players take turns drawing cards and placing cards. Player I has 86.3

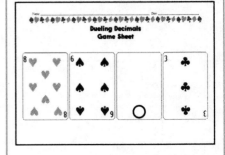

Player 2 has 94.5 and wins the round.

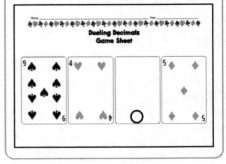

Name _____

Date _____

Dueling Decimals
Game Sheet

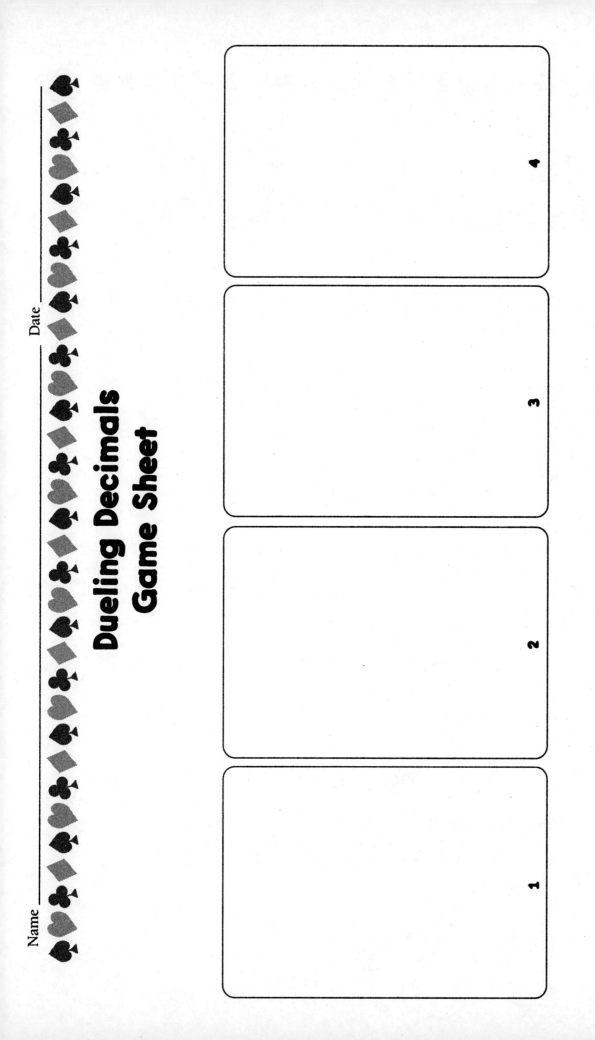

1

2

3

4

Add a Decimal

Students add
decimal numbers.

Materials

one shuffled deck of cards with tens, jokers, and face cards removed
pencils and scrap paper

The Way to Play

1 One player deals eight cards to each player and
stacks the remaining cards facedown in a pile.

2 Without looking at their cards, players place
their cards in two rows of four. Players turn
over all the cards except the third card from
the left. This card represents the decimal point.

3 Each player adds the two decimal numbers
and says the sum. The player with the greatest
sum earns 1 point.

4 Players place the used cards in a discard pile
and play another round in the same way.
When all cards have been used, the discard
pile is shuffled and used.

5 The first player to earn 10 points wins.

Example:

A player arranges the cards in two rows
and finds the sum:

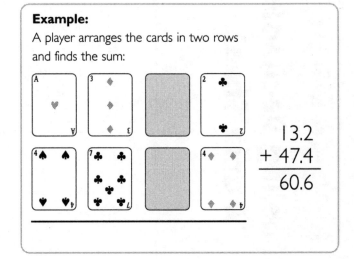

$$13.2$$
$$+ 47.4$$
$$60.6$$

♠ Variation ♣

Change the number of cards dealt or the position of the decimal
point. For example, for a more challenging game, deal 10 cards.
Arrange the cards in two rows of five and place the second card
from the left facedown to represent the decimal point.

Equation Completed!

Students follow the order of operations to create equations.

Materials

one shuffled deck of cards with jokers and face cards removed
pencils and scrap paper

The Way to Play

1. One player deals six cards to each player and stacks the remaining cards facedown in a pile. Players keep the same cards throughout the game.

2. When players are ready and have looked at their cards, one player turns over the top card and places it faceup beside the pile. This is the target card.

3. Players use any of their cards to create an expression that equals the value of the target card. Players may use any operation (addition, subtraction, multiplication, division, or any combination of operations) and must follow the order of operations (see page 5). Players may use each card only once and must use at least two of their cards.

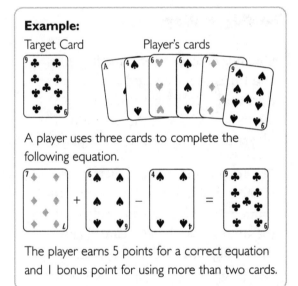

Example:

Target Card   Player's cards

A player uses three cards to complete the following equation.

The player earns 5 points for a correct equation and 1 bonus point for using more than two cards.

4. The first player to finish says, "Equation completed!" The player writes the equation while other players check it for accuracy. If correct, the player earns 5 points and the round ends. A player earns a bonus point for using more than two cards (not including the target card). If incorrect, the next round begins.

5. To begin the next round, a player turns over the next card in the pile and play continues in the same way.

6. The player with the most points after five rounds wins.

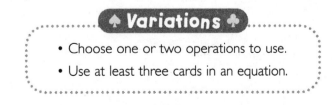

♠ **Variations** ♠

- Choose one or two operations to use.
- Use at least three cards in an equation.

Operation Rules

Students follow the order of operations to create equations.

Materials

one shuffled deck of cards with jokers and face cards removed
scrap paper and pencils

The Way to Play

1 One player stacks the cards in a pile and turns over one card. This is the start card. The player turns over a second card. This is the end card. The player deals five cards to each player.

2 Players use any or all of their cards to create a problem that begins with the number on the start card and equals the number on the end card. Players must follow the order of operations (see page 5) and may use each card only once.

3 Players write their equations on scrap paper and check each other's work.

4 If an equation is correct, a player earns 1 point for each card used and 2 points for each operation used. A player earns 5 bonus points for using all five cards.

5 At the end of the round, players return their cards, shuffle the cards, and begin a new round.

6 At the end of three rounds, the player with the most points wins.

Example:

Start Card   End Card

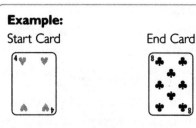

A player draws five cards.

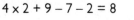

The player uses five cards to create a problem that begins with 4 and equals 8.
$$4 \times 2 + 9 - 7 - 2 = 8$$

The player scores the following points:
1 point for each card used = 4 points
2 points for each operation used
(multiplication, addition, subtraction) = 6 points
Total score for the round = 10 points

Equation Challenge

Players: 2 or more

Students follow the order of operations to create equations.

Materials

one shuffled deck of cards with jokers and face cards removed
scrap paper and pencils
calculator (optional)

The Way to Play

1 Player 1 chooses any number from 20 to 100 as the challenge number. Player 1 deals seven cards to each player. Player 1 challenges the players to use their cards to write an expression equal to the challenge number, following these guidelines:

- Players may use any of their cards and any operation, following the order of operations (see page 5). Players may use grouping symbols (parentheses).

- Players may use each card only once.

2 Players check each other's work. Players score 1 point for each card used. If a player cannot make an expression that equals the challenge number, the player does not earn any points. Players return their cards to pile.

3 Player 2 shuffles the cards, chooses a challenge number, and deals seven cards to each player.

4 The player with the most points after five (or more) rounds wins the game.

Player 1 chooses 59 as the challenge number. The player has the following cards:

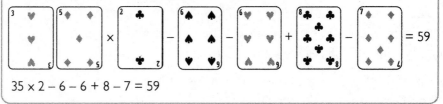

The player creates the following equation, using all seven cards.

$$35 \times 2 - 6 - 6 + 8 - 7 = 59$$

31

Computation Gridlock

Materials

one shuffled deck of cards with jokers and face cards removed
Computation Gridlock Game Sheet (page 33)
small markers that fit in the spaces on the game sheet, such as pennies, buttons, or beans
pencils and scrap paper

The Way to Play

1 One player deals seven cards to each player and stacks the remaining cards facedown in pile. Players keep the same cards throughout the game. Players place their cards faceup in a row in front of them.

2 Player 1 draws a card from the pile. Starting at the joker, Player 1 moves a marker the number of spaces indicated on the card. Players may move in any direction—up, down, sideways, or diagonally—and may switch directions, as long as the spaces touch a side or corner. Players may not backtrack through spaces that they have already passed in that turn. Players may not cross or land on the joker.

3 Player 1 reads aloud the number landed on. The player uses any or all of the seven cards to create an expression that equals the number value of the space. Players must follow the order of operations (see page 5). Player 1 writes the equation and Player 2 checks it.

4 Player 1 earns 1 point for every card used and as many points as the number of the space landed on. Player 1 leaves the marker on the space. Players may not land on or pass through this space again. If Player 1 is unable to make an expression, the player removes the marker and the turn ends. Player 1 places the card in a discard pile.

5 Player 2 takes a turn in the same way. If a player draws a card and cannot move that number of spaces, the turn ends.

6 The player with the most points after five (or more) rounds wins the game.

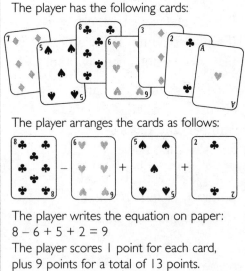

Example:
A player draws a 5 and moves 5 spaces on the game sheet.

The player has the following cards:

The player arranges the cards as follows:

The player writes the equation on paper:
$8 - 6 + 5 + 2 = 9$
The player scores 1 point for each card, plus 9 points for a total of 13 points.

Computation Gridlock
Game Sheet

5	3	7	1	4	2	8
6	10	2	3	5	7	9
1	8	4	6	10	3	4
9	7	3	🃏	3	7	9
4	3	10	6	4	8	1
9	7	5	3	2	10	6
8	2	4	1	7	3	5

Coordinate Pairs

Materials

one shuffled deck of cards with jokers and face cards removed
Coordinate Pairs Game Sheet (page 35)
two different kinds of small markers, such as beans or paper squares

The Way to Play

1 One player stacks the cards facedown in a pile and places the game
sheet on the table. Each player chooses a kind of marker.

2 Player 1 draws two cards to represent a coordinate pair. The first
card represents the x-coordinate (horizontal axis) and the second
card represents the y-coordinate (vertical axis).

3 Player 1 locates the coordinate on the game sheet, places a marker
on the coordinate, and places the cards in a discard pile.

4 Player 2 takes a turn in the same way.

5 Players continue to take turns. If an opponent's marker is already on
a coordinate, players may bump off the marker and replace it with
their own. When the cards run out, a player shuffles the discard pile
and play continues.

6 Players earn a point for placing three markers in a row—
horizontally, vertically, or diagonally. Players earn half a point for
adding a fourth or fifth marker (or more) to any three of their
markers in a row. Players do not lose points if markers are bumped.

7 The first player to earn 2 points wins.

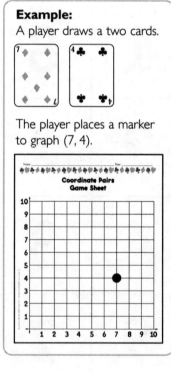

Example:
A player draws a two cards.

The player places a marker
to graph (7, 4).

♠ Variations ♣

Use a smaller grid and fewer cards, such as such as a 5 x 5 grid with cards 1–5,
or a larger grid and more cards, such as a 13 x 13 grid with cards 1–king (13).

Name _____ Date _____

Coordinate Pairs
Game Sheet

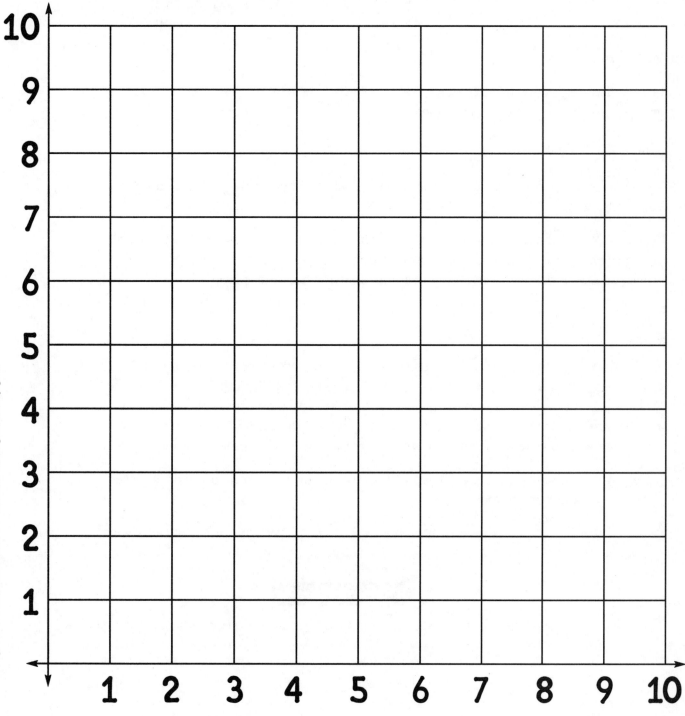

Measure Up!

Materials

one shuffled deck of cards with jokers and face cards removed
grid paper, pencils, and erasers (optional)

The Way to Play

1 One player deals five cards to each player and stacks the remaining cards facedown in a pile.

2 Player 1 draws the top card without showing it to the other player. This card represents length. Player 1 then chooses a card from his or her hand to represent width. The player places these cards together facedown without showing the other player.

3 Player 2 takes a turn in the same way.

4 Players turn over their cards and calculate the area using the formula $A = L \times W$. The player with the greater area collects the four cards and places them in a separate pile. If players have the same area, players set the cards aside and begin the next round. The player who wins the next round wins all eight cards. (For additional reinforcement of skills, have students each draw their shape on graph paper and find the perimeter as well as area of the shape. The player with the greater area collects the cards.)

5 Play continues in the same way. When players use all the cards in their hands, a player deals five more cards to each player.

6 The game ends when all the cards have been used. The player with the most cards wins.

♠ Variation ♣

Use face cards to represent the numbers 11 (jack), 12 (queen), and 13 (king).

36

Possible Chances

Students convert fractions to percents as they predict the chances of drawing certain cards.

Materials

one shuffled deck of cards with jokers removed
Possible Chances Game Sheet, one per player (page 38)
pencils and erasers

NOTE: This game is designed for older students.

The Way to Play

1 Player 1 stacks the cards facedown in a pile and draws two cards.

2 Player 1 crosses out the two cards on the game sheet. The player then circles all the cards that have the same value as the cards drawn or that fall between the two card values.

3 Player 1 figures out the chances of the next card drawn being one of the circled cards. The player fills out the game sheet, following the example at right.

4 Player 1 predicts whether or not the next card will be one of the circled numbers. The player draws a card and scores 1 point if the prediction was correct. The player returns all the cards to the deck, shuffles it, and the turn ends.

5 Player 2 takes a turn in the same way.

6 Play continues until each player had filled in the three boxes on the game sheet. Before each turn begins, players erase the numbers circled at the top of the game sheet.

7 The player with the most points at the end of the game wins.

Example:

Player 1 draws a 6 of diamonds and a queen of hearts.

The player crosses out these two cards and circles all the cards with the same value or between the two values.

The player fills in the game sheet.

Name _____ Date _____

Possible Chances Game Sheet

♥	1	2	3	4	5	⑥	⑦	⑧	⑨	⑩	Ⓙ	Q̶	K
♦	1	2	3	4	5	6̶	⑦	⑧	⑨	⑩	Ⓙ	Q	K
♠	1	2	3	4	5	⑥	⑦	⑧	⑨	⑩	Ⓙ	Q	K
♣	1	2	3	4	5	⑥	⑦	⑧	⑨	⑩	Ⓙ	Q	K

Number of cards drawn	2
Number of cards circled	26
Number of cards left in the deck	50
Fraction representing circled cards	26/50
Fraction representing the percent of circled cards	52 /100
Percent of chance	52%

The player predicts that the next card will be one of the circled cards. The player draws a 7 and scores a point.

♠ Variation ♣

For a less challenging game, have students leave the shaded sections blank.

Possible Chances Game Sheet

♥	1	2	3	4	5	6	7	8	9	10	J	Q	K
♦	1	2	3	4	5	6	7	8	9	10	J	Q	K
♠	1	2	3	4	5	6	7	8	9	10	J	Q	K
♣	1	2	3	4	5	6	7	8	9	10	J	Q	K

Number of cards drawn	
Number of cards circled	
Number of cards left in the deck	
Fraction representing circled cards	
Fraction representing the percent of circled cards	/ 100
Percent of chance	

Number of cards drawn	
Number of cards circled	
Number of cards left in the deck	
Fraction representing circled cards	
Fraction representing the percent of circled cards	/ 100
Percent of chance	

Number of cards drawn	
Number of cards circled	
Number of cards left in the deck	
Fraction representing circled cards	
Fraction representing the percent of circled cards	/ 100
Percent of chance	

Magic Card Squares

Students add, subtract, and build problem-solving skills as they create Magic Squares.

Materials

Magic Card Squares Game Sheet, one per player (page 40)

For a magic square with sums of
12—four of each: joker (0), ace (1), 2, 3, 4, 5, 6, 7, 8
15—four of each: ace (1), 2, 3, 4, 5, 6, 7, 8, 9
18—four of each: 2, 3, 4, 5, 6, 7, 8, 9, 10
21—four of each: 3, 4, 5, 6, 7, 8, 9, 10, 11 (jack)
24—four of each: 4, 5, 6, 7, 8, 9, 10, 11 (jack), 12 (queen)

Before playing, explain that a magic square is made up of nine numbers. The sum of each side—horizontal, vertical, and diagonal—is the same. Review the steps at right for creating magic squares.

The Way to Play

1 Players decide which Magic Square sum they will use: 12, 15, 18, 21, or 24. Players select the cards needed (see above), shuffle them, and stack them facedown.

2 Player 1 draws the top card. If the player wishes to use the card anywhere in the magic square, the player places the card in a box on the game sheet and the turn ends. If the player does not want to use the card, the player places the card in a discard pile and the turn ends. The other players take turns in the same way.

3 Players continue to take turns. To move a card, a player must use a turn without drawing a card. Players shuffle and use the discard pile as needed. The first player to complete the magic square successfully wins.

12

7	0	5
2	4	6
3	8	1

15

8	1	6
3	5	7
4	9	2

18

9	2	7
4	6	8
5	10	3

21

10	3	8
5	7	9
6	11	4

24

11	4	9
6	8	10
7	12	5

How to Create a Magic Square:

These steps work for any magic square. The example uses the magic square for 15.

1. Divide the sum of the Magic Square by 3 to find the center number. For example: to find the center number of a Magic Square of 15, divide 15 by 3 (5). Write 5 in the center square.

2. Add 1 to the center square (5 + 1) and write the sum (6) in the top right corner. Subtract 1 from the center square (5 − 1) and write the difference (4) in bottom left corner.

3. Add 2 to the center square (5 + 2) and write the sum (7) to the right of the center square. Subtract 2 from the center square (5 − 2) and write the difference (3) to the left of the center square.

4. Add 3 to the center square (5 + 3) and write the sum (8) in the top left corner. Subtract 3 from the center square (5 − 3) and write the difference (2) in the bottom right corner.

5. Add 4 to the center square (5 + 4) and write the sum (9) directly under the 5. Subtract 4 from 5 (5 − 4) and write the difference (1) directly above the 5.

Magic Card
Squares
Game Sheet

Card Detective

Students use problem-solving strategies and logical reasoning to solve a card-placement mystery.

Materials
♦♦♦♦♦♦♦♦♦

Card Detective Game Sheet, one per player (page 42)
pencils
reproducible cards, one set of six per player (pages 43–48, optional)
red crayon or marker (optional)

NOTE: This game is designed for older students.

The Way to Play
♦♦♦♦♦♦♦♦♦♦♦♦♦♦♦

1) Give each student a pencil and a game sheet. You may wish to reproduce for each child the cards mentioned in this problem. Have students color the hearts and diamonds red, then cut out the cards, and use them as manipulatives.

2) Explain that they have six cards: 3 of clubs, 4 of hearts, 5 of hearts, 7 of diamonds, 8 of spades, and 10 of spades. (Place the six cards facedown in a row to help students visualize the problem.) Explain that students will use clues to determine the correct order of the six cards. The six places are numbered 1 to 6, from left to right.

3) Read the clues together with students. (You may want to create an overhead transparency of the game sheet.) Show students how to draw an X in each box when they have eliminated a card from a particular position. Instruct students to draw a star in a box when the clues reveal the correct position for a particular card. Lead students to use a process of elimination to work through the problem. If needed, remind students that when they draw a star in a space, they can eliminate that position as a possibility for the other cards.

Solution:

41

Card Detective Game Sheet

Read the clues below to figure out the correct order of the six cards. The places are numbered 1 to 6 from left to right. Write an X in a box to show that a card does not belong in a space. Draw a star in a box to show that a card does belong in a space. Once you have finished, write the number of the cards in the correct order at the bottom of the page.

Clues

1. There are three red cards in a row.

2. The 8 of spades and the 7 of diamonds are on the ends.

3. The 5 of hearts is two cards before the 7 of diamonds.

4. The 10 of spades is not next to the 5 of hearts.

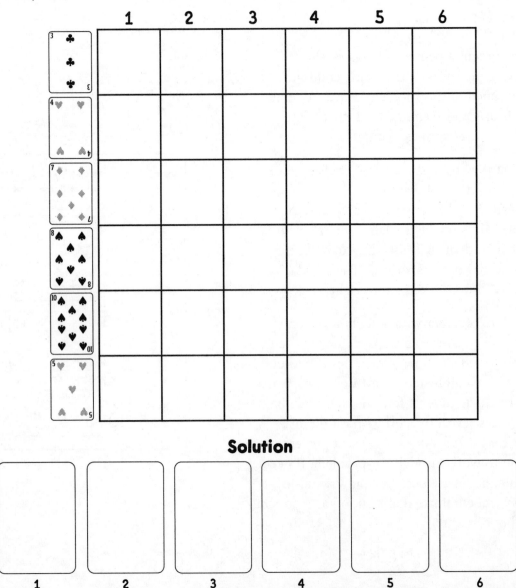

Solution

1   2   3   4   5   6

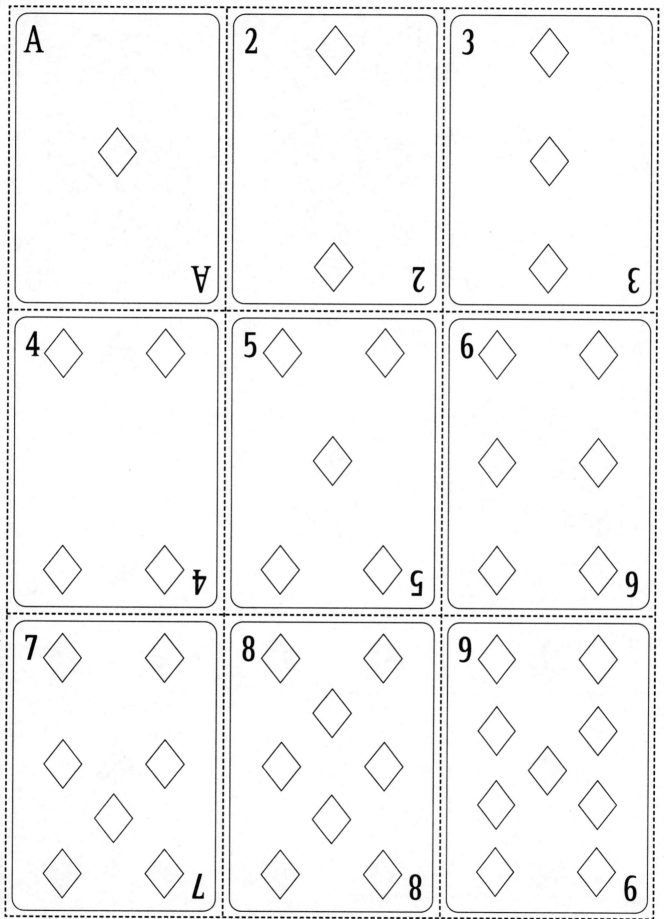

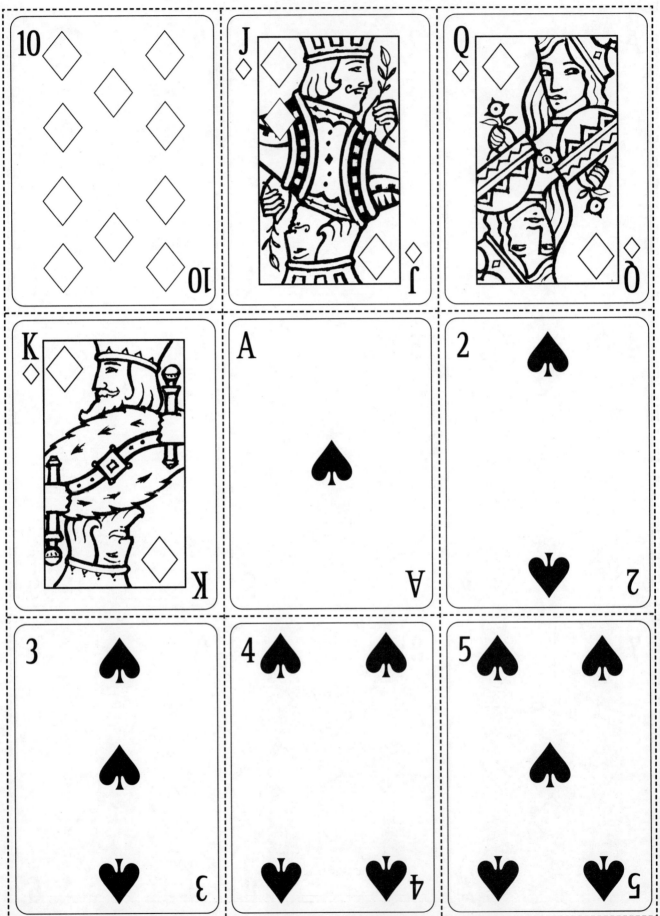

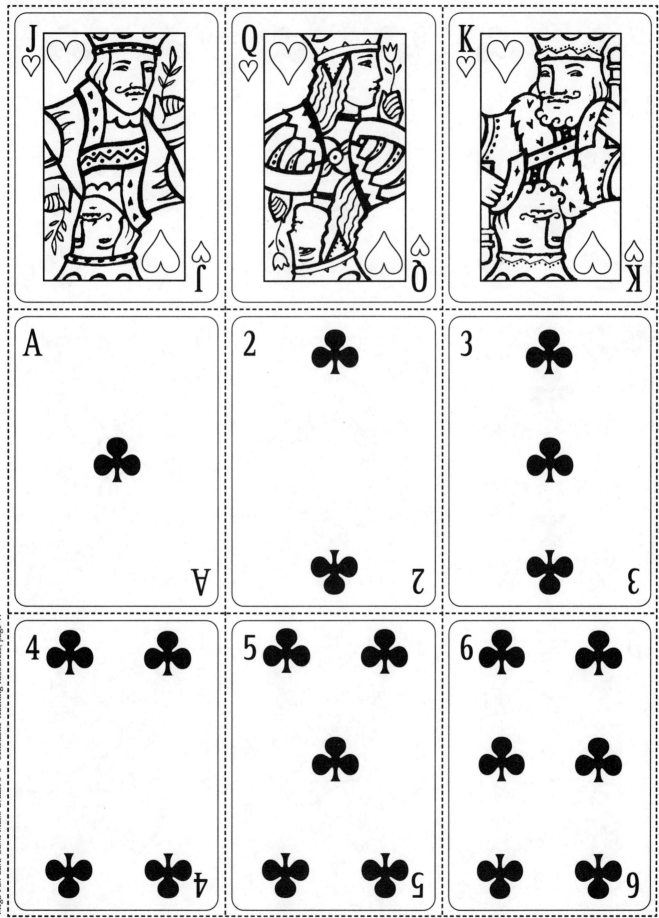

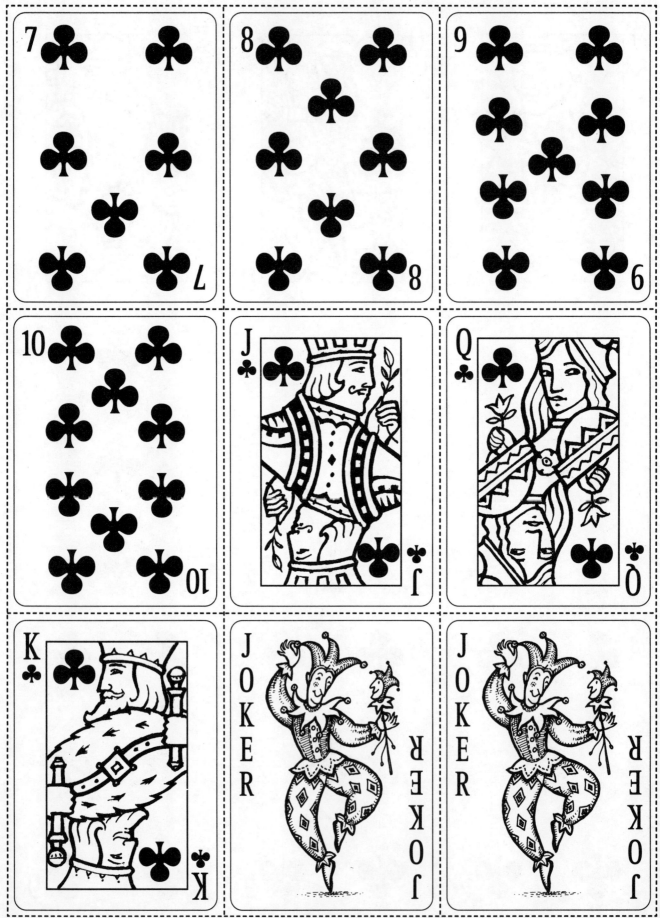